WAS THE WEST REALLY WON BY
HORSES & WOMEN?

Poems,

Stories,

and

Prayers

by

ROY K. HALL, SR.

Out of South Fork

An imprint of MJS Publishing Group, LLC

Colorado

2007

Copyright 2007 by Roy K. Hall, Sr.

All rights reserved. No part of this book may be reproduced in any form or by an electronic or mechanical means including information storage and retrieval systems without permission in writing from the publisher, except by a reviewer who may quote passages in a review.

Printed in the United States of America

Published by
MJS Publishing Group, LLC
PO Box 505
Monte Vista, Colorado 81144
www.mjspub.com

ISBN: 0-9764336-5-6

Cover design & typesetting by
Ignite Communications & Design, Inc.

Typeset in Minion and Captain Howdy.

Cover artist: Phil Epp
Painting:: *Windy Hill*
Courtesy of Platt Fine Art, LLC
www.plattfineart.com

TABLE OF CONTENT

POEMS

Morning	8
Just Listen	9
Tears Falling	11
Spring	12
Charlie Evans	13
Ropin' a Pig	15
The Old Men and the Steer	20
Burrs	22
Sand, Cattle, and Men	24
Mares at Feeding Time	27
Darrell Biggerstaff	28
Cowboy at the Rodeo	29
Old Saddles	30
Circle C	32
Talking With God	34
The Mule from Round Mountain	36
Life	38
Hurt Someone	39
Cowboy Who Didn't Know	40
Love Is New	42
Hiedi	43
Mikayla	44
Christmas	45
Two Old Men	46
Back When	47
Little Katy	48
Ethan	49
Growing Up Fast	50
Grandkids	51
Ed Covey	52
The Colt and the Old Cowboy's Prayer	53
Cowboy Life	55

SHORT STORIES

Breaking Colts 58
The Jackass, Sam, and Me 60
Gathering Cattle for the Bank 62

PRAYERS

Traveling Prayer 66
Cowboy Lookin' for a Wife 67
Horse Prayer 69
A Cowboy Who Finds His Love 70
A Farmer's Prayer 71
A Cowboy's Prayer for His Wife 72
Talkin' With the Lord 73
Another Day 74
A Cowboy on the Range 75
Mercy 76

ABOUT THE AUTHOR 79

POEMS

MORNING

It is so quiet
This time of day,
Morning breaks and
The sun shines 'cross the way.

No sound of people
And all that fuss,
Just God and his angels
Looking down on us.

What a way
To start one's day,
And to think God made us
From but a lump of clay.

How amazing is life
And what it has to give,
Like this beautiful morning
And how God has let us live.

JUST LISTEN

A time to just
Sit and listen,
You hear the wind
Just a-hissin'.

Blowin' cool
Upon this spring night,
Makes it feel like all is good
And everything is right.

God smiles and looks down
Upon this land,
Taking care of each and every one
Of these things called man.

God placed us here
To care for what is His,
But as men we fail
And that seems the way it is.

But God forgives us
And lets us go on,
'Cause He loves us
And will till the day we're gone.

If we could only do as our Father does
With unconditional love,
With forgiveness in our hearts
Like that sent from God above.

Since time began God's been patient
In this place we call home,
He gives us a chance to do
What's right, as time is His alone.

So build your house
Upon the rock and not the sand,
And remember we are only here
Because it's part of God's plan.

TEARS FALLING

Tears fall
From a single broken heart,
For love
Takes two, doin' their part.

Without this kind
And gentle care,
Love is just a word
Floating on air.

So never look down
On the one you love,
Because love doesn't always fit
Like a fine satin glove.

SPRING

I see the old hill is just about bare,
Soon green grass will be puttin' up everywhere.

Spring rains will come
And all the little creeks will be on the run.

The sun will shine from high up above—
It's spring, and God is sending us His love.

CHARLIE EVANS

Now there's old Charlie Evans
A dear ol' friend of mine,
He's been bucked off mules
Many, many times.

Charlie's a hog hunter
Like few men have seen,
He's killed a few
That were pretty darn mean.

He once had a bear
Taking up his back yard,
He tried to hang it,
But it was just too hard.

So he decided
To keep it around,
He'd have something to run
With his flop-eared hound.

His poor wife—
What a sight to see,
She put up with a man
Like good ol' Charlie.

I don't know
If Charlie ever worked anywhere,
And I doubt if
He ever really gave a care.

But he's my buddy
And a real good friend,
And I'll bet he'll be the same
Till the time his days end.

ROPIN' A PIG

One time I was riding pasture,
About 25 years ago,
Down in southern Oklahoma
Where the old Washita River flows.

I dropped off a hill
Near a little old creek,
As I rode along I thought
I could hear some pigs squeal and squeak.

My ol' pony had never seen a pig
Let alone heard one.
What we didn't know was
We were gonna get an education, bar none.

As we rode along that little creek
It came out into a cornfield.
I could see where the hogs had been
And thought, "I can rope one, if the ol' pony will."

By now we were close enough
The pony could smell them,
He's a-snortin' and runnin' backwards—
Hell, he thought they were going to eat him.

I kept a-spurrin'
And nursin' him along,
I was a-thinkin', "If he sees these pigs
He may be long gone."

But being the cowboy
That I am at this time,
He's about to run away
And I got ropin' on my mind.

All at once
All hell breaks loose.
These pigs run out and my pony takes off
Like an old scared goose.

Hell, they caught me by surprise
And almost messed up my loop.
If he had hung on a little longer
I'd have caught one with a single scoop.

By this time hogs were runnin' everywhere
Since my pony spooked them, you see.
I wanted to rope one, but for him
This just wasn't going to be.

Hell, he was about to mess up my concentration
With all that buckin' and squealin'
He must have known my limitation.

Being a cow horse I knew
He had it in him to built right to that pig,
But with his jumpin' and a-snortin'
I must have looked like a preacher about to lose his wig.

I finally over-and-undered
Him a time or two,
And put his mind on pigs
When I was through.

We finally got one out in the open
And boy could he fly.
I was a-thinking, "If I don't get him roped
We can kiss his hams goodbye."

Don't ever let anyone tell you
Ropin' pigs is fun,
I am here to tell you
Those damn things can run.

Poor ol' Buster
Was givin' it all he had,
Hell, that pig must have looked like a kid
A-runnin' from his dad.

I was tied on hard and fast
And lookin' for that loop,
Little did I know
That pigs could do more than grunt and poop.

As that pig turned back
And I passed him by,
Ol' Buster put the brakes on
And out of the saddle I did fly.

A-slidin' through that plowed earth
On my face and knees,
Ol' Buster was standin' there lookin'
As if he might actually be pleased.

I said, "Come here, you worthless thing
And help me get up on your ass.
We're going to catch that pig
'Cause I know he ain't all that fast."

This ol' pig
Seemed to be a-waitin' on us,
'Cause he was just standing out in the field
A-watchin' me cuss.

I told ol' Buster,
"We'll get him this time,
And when we do
Them pork chops will taste mighty fine."

So we built to him
Like nothing you've ever seen,
When I put the loop on him, he didn't weigh but 125—
But this ol' hog was mean.

Fought like no cow I ever saw,
He felt to me like he was 10-foot tall.

There's no one around
So I am a-talkin' to my horse,
"You know, we got to kill this thing, of course."

But, hell, he didn't want to die
As we were draggin' him,
He still had fight in his eye.

I told ol' Buster, "This thing is a-stinkin'
Like something you ought not to smell.
Let's take him through the creek
And give him a bath, as well."

He never quit a-fightin'
All the way back to my home,
We thought we had him secured—
Next morning the ol' pig was gone.

I was a-tellin' my wife about this pig ropin' thing
And all we'd been through,
And all she had to say is,
"That's all you had to do?"

She must not have understood
'Cause all I was saying
Was Buster and me,
Hell, we're damn good.

THE OLD MEN AND THE STEER

We were runnin' wheat cattle—
It was springtime at the Bar C.
There were three of us,
Two old men and me.

We got the call one ev'nin'
Down along the Washita,
Prices had gone up,
We had to gather them all.

We had 'em headed for the lots
When I heard ol' Ike yell,
They were headed for the river,
As far as he could tell.

I had the fastest horse,
I headed for the flank,
I looked up and saw ol' Ike,
Headed for the riverbank.

The steer turned right past him,
Ike looked at me and grinned,
He pulled his rope down and
I'm thinkin', "Here we go again."

Ike tossed the rope on him
As the steer passed him by,
Then I saw his girt was busted,
Ike was sailin' toward the sky.

I guess he'd been there a time or two,
'Cause takin' just a few
He comes with his knife
Then the cowboy and rope flew.

And so I end this story
I have so gracefully told,
About a cowboy
Who never got too old.

BURRS

It was Ike, Gud, and me,
The old hands and me were out riding pasture, you see.

We ran cattle down along the Washita—
It was the damnedest place you ever saw.

Those cows would hide in the cane breaks to get out of the cold,
The old hands asked me to get 'em out because they were too dang old.

They had used this line on me so many times,
I was beginning to think they liked to mess with my mind.

Those two old men weren't dumb,
They just liked to use me 'cause I was young.

They thought they'd see a show out of me,
'Cause my ol' pony would buck when it was cold, you see.

Later on as we went through the day,
I found a patch of cockleburs as we rode along the way.

I grabbed a handful and when Ike and Gud stopped for a smoke,
I put the burrs 'neath their saddles—just for a joke.

Oh boy, you should have seen the show,
It was a thrill just to see that old buckskin blow.

Gud was hangin' up there in the sky,
Bluebirds could have built a nest underneath this guy.

Ike's old horse he'd buck and he'd spin,
Bringin' ol' Ike back to earth again.

It was all worth the show and I'd do it again,
Just to see the looks on the faces of these two old men.

Well, I caught their horses and took the burrs from their saddles,
If they knew what I'd done we would have had a battle.

I never told them what I did that day
'Cause they would have shot me and left me where I lay.

SAND, CATTLE, AND MEN

Now we were pushin' cattle,
A long, long time ago.
Down along the Red River
Where the muddy waters flow.

We were working for the Chapmans
Up on their big ol' spread,
Thousand and thousands of acres
Along the old Big Red.

Now we had been ridin'
It seems a day or two,
When finally we found the cattle
We knew just what to do.

We would push the cattle yonder,
Across meadows, through pine so tall,
Across the sandy beaches
And up the muddy draw.

Some of these cattle hadn't seen a man
In their whole danged lives,
And when we came out of the brush
Their first thought was to survive.

They took to runnin' and scattered
Cattle goin' left and right.
It looked like we'd be runnin' cattle
All through that dark cold night.

We fell right in behind them
Tryin' to do our best.
But these cattle were wild
Sure 'nuf puttin' us to the test.

Men and dogs and horses and cattle
All over the place
You just had to have been there,
It was a hell of a race.

We ran them through the Bodarks
And out the other side.
Hell, I never seen so many cattle
With so many places to hide.

You were always lookin' for a clearing,
Or an opening up ahead
And just a-hopin' you and your trusty
Horse didn't wind up dead.

Now, I have run some cattle
Across this land of ours.
But I ain't never seen nothin'
Like those Texas briars.

You could ride in those briar patches
And out the other side,
And if you were lucky
You might still have your hide.

Those old cows weren't dumb
They had done this time and again,
Out-smartin' cowboys
Till there was no end.

I never really knew
How many cattle there was down there,
But if I had it to do again
I'd stay home in my rockin' chair.

MARES AT FEEDING TIME

The mares are a-standin'
At the gate,
A-waitin' on feed
And I'm a little bit late.

They stand and wait
Each and every day,
They've become accustomed
To me feedin' 'em this way.

When I was a boy years ago,
My dad's mules would stand and wait
To see my dad with the feed bucket
Enter the gate.

These ol' mares remind me
Of days gone by,
As I watch them pace
It brings a tear to my eye.

'Cause it's the life
And times of old,
Our childhood memories
That never get cold.

It's feedin' time
For the mind and soul.
Like the mules and mares
Memories retold.

DARRELL BIGGERSTAFF

Now there's
Old Darrell Biggerstaff,
Not a big man—
Maybe half.

He's a muleskinner
Like you've rarely seen,
He can make them move faster
Than any machine.

The guy is truly
A sight to behold,
He likes to help
But he's stoved up and not that old.

He walks a good walk and talks a good talk
But I must say,
When it comes to working
Darrell ain't gonna get in the way.

He's not scared of work
This is plain to see,
He could lie down right beside it
'Neath the shade of a tree.

Oh, I like to have a little fun
With him I guess,
But when it comes to men
Darrell's one of the best.

COWBOY AT THE RODEO

I heard a cowboy pray one time…

"If this bull bucks me off
And breaks me half in two,
God, don't forget me
'Cause I'll be thinkin' of you.

You have always been with me
No matter how hard the ride,
It always felt like you were sitting there
Right by my side."

I thought about
What he had to say
As he put in a damn good ride
On the bull that day.

When the ride was over
And he walked away,
I heard another guy
To the cowboy say:

"Do you really think God was with you
on that bull today?"

The cowboy turned around
And with a glow on his face,
Answered him, "I know
'Cause I was saved by His amazing grace."

OLD SADDLES

Old saddles
Have stories untold,
About many a cowboy
That's been bucked off and throwed.

Saddles are something
Every cowboy can talk about,
A saddle is something
They will never be without.

Good saddles
Are hard to find,
They don't make them
Like they did in olden times.

Hereford and Bonny Allen
Were the best you could find,
You could buy one
Anywhere, anytime.

Now they're not handmade
But built on an assembly line,
Some are nice—
If you like that kind.

They use plastic
And fiberglass, you see,
But to me, ain't nothing
Like a rawhide cover on a wooden tree.

I guess I could go on
About old saddles 'most all night,
Myself I like the old ones
'Cause they were built just right.

CIRCLE C

Here's to the horse
That pulls the wagon—
'Cause I'm a-ridin'
And not a-draggin'.

Here's to the people
Who ride along—
And to all of those
Singin' a happy song.

It makes the trail
Seem awfully sweet—
'Cause we know before long
We'll stop and eat.

Then with our backs
To the wind,
We'll mount up
And ride again.

It gives our guests a story to tell
Of a day well spent,
And how much fun we had
And how the day has went.

This would be the cowboy life
For some you see,
We are here so they can have some fun—
This I guarantee.

So enjoy yourself,
If you please,
We're so happy to have you
Here at the Circle C.

TALKING WITH GOD

There once was a cowboy who rode up a mountain
And fell to his knees,
He prayed and suddenly heard God speaking
Through the leaves.

He said to God,
"How high must I ride
To reach the heavens
And take a look inside?"

God answered the cowboy and said,
"Be sure your spurs are shiny,
And clean your boots of old,
Because I need more cowboys
Walking my streets of gold."

Then the cowboy asked,
"How must I get there? My horse can't run on air."
God said, "Be patient
And I'll send you a golden stair."

Again the cowboy asked,
"When must I climb those stairs so high?"
God answered him and said,
"My son you start the day you die."

Just then the cowboy felt
A cool mist upon his face,
And realized that God
Was here and in every place.

The cowboy said,
"I'm so glad to be a child of yours,
And before I die I hope to do a better job
Helping you with your chores."

God answered,
"I'd be proud to have you ride along,
'Cause without cowboys like you,
Many souls would be lost and gone.

THE MULE FROM ROUND MOUNTAIN

I was sitting on the front porch starin' down the road,
When I saw my old red mule that needed to be rode.
I was just thinkin' how he could take me for a ride
Across that old mountain and down the other side.

Then I saw someone a-comin' in a nice red truck,
"Man," I'm thinkin', "that's just my luck."
They were pullin' a nice red trailer, in fact,
So nice it was I thought the old mule would attack.

They pulled right up the drive, asked if I wanted to go for a ride,
I said, "Yes I do; I need to ride that red mule, the ornery old hide."
It seemed like forever but about an hour later,
We finally got him loaded in that nice red trailer.

Soon we were all on our way,
Me, I'm a-thinkin', "Lord, don't let him buck today."
We get to the bottom of the hill,
And I'm still asking, "Lord, don't let me take a spill."

As we unloaded down the road a piece,
I heard them laughing and making fun of my old beast.
I told them, "This old mule is fast—
Three-quarters horse and one-quarter ass—

When we hit the mountain, you boys are going to see,
This old mule can climb the mountain like a coon climbs a tree."
I think they thought I was poking fun at them and their rides,
They took off and left me alone standing on the roadside.

When I caught up it was steep, too steep for a horse to climb,
My old mule just passed them leaving everyone behind.
The mule and I had gone all the way to the top,
But me I didn't see the thirty-foot drop.

They were coming up in back of me when I heard one yell,
"It's too steep! My horse done went and fell."
So they all turned and left me standing on top of the hill,
My mule was getting lonely and wouldn't stand still.

We made it to the top of this old hump,
Little did I know the mule was about to jump.
He was eyeballin' a thirty-foot bluff,
And I'm a-thinkin' this mule ain't that tough.

But off the bluff we went thirty feet in the air,
I am lookin' toward the heavens, "Dear Lord, I hope you care."
We hit the ground a-slidin' and as far as I could see,
That old mule was flyin' and he was draggin' me.

The boys below was laughin' and poking fun at me,
I guess I should have never said that mule could climb a tree.
I thought that mule had gone and left me kind of stuck,
But there he was waitin' by the pickup truck.

It's all over, said, and done,
I guess we all had some pretty big fun.
The boys will never let me forget that day,
When my mule dumped me and went on his way.

LIFE

My life here is oh so fast,
My journey's just about done.
I would like to say it's been good,
And I had a lot of fun.

Thank you, Lord, for this life,
And the way it all come.
I am glad that's it's over, Lord,
It's been quite the run.

HURT SOMEONE

I found out today
How wrong I have been,
I've seen someone I love
Eaten up with guilt and sin.

As I talk with her and see what she's become,
It makes me feel so cold inside.
To know that it was my fault,
Makes me want to hide.

The pain she feels
For what she has done,
She only wants to find
A place to hide and run.

God forgive us, show us how to love again
And leave behind the past,
Our lives, it seems,
Are running out of time all too fast.

The final wages of sin is death
And we've not far to go,
But if we look to you, Lord, for forgiveness
Then who are we to know?

COWBOY WHO DIDN'T KNOW

A cowboy was alone one day,
His wife had up and went away—
Leavin' him with a broken heart—
He'd messed up and not done his part.

How to keep his life and wife together
He had no idea at all.
He knew he'd messed up
When she asked him not to make the call.

All she wanted him to be
Was a husband and her lover true.
But he didn't see the signs
And soon they were through.

She loved this cowboy
There was no doubt,
But his messin' around
She could do without.

It may not have been
As it seemed to his wife,
But when he didn't listen
He screwed up his life.

So now he's alone
And the loss hard to bear,
'Cause he never let her know
How much he really cared.

He now sits
And cries alone
'Cause of all the reminders
In this place they once called home.

How he wishes
That he had done right by his wife,
'Cause when she left
She took the biggest part of his life.

But being a man that he is
He lost the wife who once was his.
But life goes on, this is true,
It happened to him, it could happen to you.

"Cowboy up," they say,
But these people never lost
The best thing to come their way.

LOVE IS NEW

As time goes by
So do we,
I feel our love is as strong
As any love can be.

With our hearts
So full of love,
We face each day with a feeling
Sent only from above.

So take my heart
And gladly I will give it my best,
To love you forever
And never put us to the test.

For, my love,
This is what life's all about,
I believe God has sent you to me,
I have no doubts.

So love me
While you can,
But never forget
I'm not a saint, I'm just a man.

HIEDI

Today I saw
A special little girl,
You could tell
She was a part of her nanny's world.

Her little smile
Was so soft and sweet,
Oh, how she got around
On those tiny little feet.

I watched her go
Here and there,
As her nanny chased her
Around everywhere.

She was such a sight to see,
Made me wish she
And her nanny belonged to me.

As I looked at this baby
So soft and sweet,
I knew only God could make one
So innocent and complete.

Thanks to nanny
For bringing her by,
'Cause she reminds me of my Katie
And brings a tear to this ol' cowboy's eye.

MIKAYLA

Mikayla is my granddaughter
As sweet as she can be,
She's the third little girl
My kids brought home, you see.

I don't know
What makes her so sweet,
Maybe it's her fat little rolls
Or those tiny little feet.

God has a way with grandkids—
Just making them grand,
I guess it's just to fill
The heart of this old man.

But as a Papa
I can truly say,
This baby's made Papa's world
A better place to stay.

I love you, Mikayla, as I do all my grandkids.

CHRISTMAS

What does Christmas mean to me?

It means a baby was born
A long time ago, you see.
This is the meaning
Of Christmas to me.

He came to die
For all our sins,
Then He arose
And came back again.

Christmas
Is a good time of year,
It fills one's heart
With love and cheer.

In this world
That moves so fast,
It's good to look
Back on the past.

To the precious baby
That came for you and me,
That's why there's love
'Neath the Christmas tree.

So take a gift
From beneath the Christmas tree,
Then think of the gift
God gave you and me.

TWO OLD MEN

I was feeding cattle
And ridin' fence out west,
With two old men who showed me respect.
Little did I know I was workin' with the best.

I've seen them rope cattle
And I've seen how they ride.
These men rode like statues,
Silently, side by side.

They are there when you need them
For a laugh or a joke,
These were cowboys,
They were true cowpokes.

I hope when I'm ridin' fences
Up there in the sky,
These two are ridin' with me
In the sweet by and by.

BACK WHEN

Back when times were good and clean—
The good old days—
Back before the machine,

Back in the days when it was done by horse,
Back when a man's word
Meant something, of course,

Back when neighbors would lend you a hand,
Back in the days
When you'd return the favor when you can.

We all called 'em the good ol' days.
But times were a-changin'
And so were our ways.

No time for neighbors, or none of that stuff,
We all go too fast
Never seem to get enough.

But it's nice to look back and to recall,
The good old days
And how we loved 'em all.

LITTLE KATY

My little Katy,
She's a sight to see,
A-ridin' that big ol' horse
And makin' a wreck out of me.

She rides like a big girl,
Makes us all look on in fear,
'Cause this little cowgirl's tiny,
She's only in her third year.

If she keeps this up, she will be
The best you ever saw.
'Cause when it comes to horses
She's always on the ball.

She may cry and fuss with her mama,
And tell her a thing or two.
But when it comes to ol' Dollar,
She's a cowgirl through and through.

She and that horse are buddies,
This is plain to see.
'Cause no one can handle ol' Dollar
Like my little Katy.

Ol' Dollar once was mine
But I lost him to this little one.
'Cause lookin' in his eyes he's havin'
With Katy a lot more fun.

ETHAN

Ethan is my grandson
And may never walk at all.

But he's still my grandson,
I love him as if he were ten-foot tall.

I'm proud of my grandson,
I want everyone to see

The smile God has given him—
He means so much to me.

I love you, little guy.

GROWING UP FAST

It was in the fall of '75
I was workin' for the KFR
And tryin' to survive.

I had a wife about to have a son.
Little did I know
That life had just begun.

I was soon to be a daddy—
Or soon become a man—
But I was still a boy
It was hard to understand.

I had so many things I needed to do.
Now that I am a man,
I've narrowed it down to just a few.

Time goes by faster each and every day.
I'm talking to Dad
Tryin' to learn his way.

For he raised a family,
A big one at its best.
He knew how to make a livin'
How it put a man to the test.

I hope I brought my dad a little joy.
But now I've got to go
And try to raise this little boy.

GRANDKIDS

Grandkids are so special
As sweet as they can be.
I love to spoil them rotten
And send them home to thee.

ED COVEY

Now there's old Ed Covey,
Quite a sight to see,
He's went and got old
And just wants to be let be.

Yes, he's had some good times
A cowboyin' in his past,
But his cowboy days are over
The rockin' chair's a-creepin' up fast.

Horses were his speciality,
On this I must say,
He could take a colt from A to Z,
And do it all in one day.

Yes, ol' Ed has been my buddy
And we've had our ups and downs.
He's laughed at me many a time,
When my ol' butt hit the ground.

THE COLT AND THE OLD COWBOY'S PRAYER

In the spring of the colt's third year,
I decided it was time to ride.
I thought I'd take him for spin,
'Round the mountainside.

I put him in the round pen
And threw the saddle on him,
Then much to my surprise,
He bucked off the saddle and kicked dirt in my eyes.

I knew he was gonna be a bad one,
For I've seen me quite a few.
If I could only get the saddle on him
I thought I could ride him a week or two.

So I tied him off to Dollar
And started up the hill,
If I could drag him to the top,
He might be movin' pretty slow.

Now Dollar is his daddy—
A better horse there's never been.
I'm thinkin' I'll slide off Dollar,
Right over on to him

But he must have been asleep,
'Cause when I hit the saddle
Over the top of Dollar
He bucked with all four feet.

I'm lookin' for a place to get off,
But it all looks the same.
He bucks right back to Dollar—
To him it's just a game.

He's bucking straight,
This I can plainly see.
This colt's goin' to the house—
With me or without me.

About that time I see ol' Dollar
Standing by the road,
Thank you, Lord, for sending him
To help me with this load.

The colt came back to Dollar,
And stopped to make a spin.
I slid out of the saddle,
And back onto Dollar again.

The days have come and gone
Since that colt bucked with me up there.
I'll never forget ol' Dollar
And God answering this cowboy's prayer.

COWBOY LIFE

The days are long, the nights are cold,
Out here with the cows can make a man feel old.

We drive them all day, set with them all night,
Freezing our asses off till morning light.

We are so tired and alone,
We still got a month till we're finally home.

Oh, but it's the cowboy way,
Following cows, smelling shit all day.

I wish I had another trade.
Maybe I'd have time to set in the shade.

I'd have a wife who loves me dear,
And we'd have a kid each and every year.

Hell, I must be nuts to want these things,
Look how much trouble the good life brings!

A wife and kids, oh what a mess that'd be,
I don't even like cows a-countin' on me.

Guess I'll stick with the cows and horses and such,
That family life is askin' just too damn much.

SHORT STORIES

BREAKING COLTS

A few years back, a friend and I were breaking colts in the Rockies. We had been there for a week or so and were pushin' these ponies pretty hard. The weather was nice—the days were warm, the nights just a little cool, and we woke up in the morning with a little frost on our sleeping bags.

I'd get up every morning and fix breakfast while my partner saddled up the ponies, and we'd get an early start. We tried to put ten miles a day on these colts and did it for thirty days.

This one morning we started out and things seemed to be going fine. Not a whole lot of bucking—just the normal stuff out of colts. We came up on this narrow trail, just abut three feet wide. It was walled straight up on one side and straight down on the other with nowhere to go but forward.

We had ten colts tied head to tail. We were riding two and leading eight, trying to pack the ones we didn't ride. This was the start of our third week, and we hadn't really seen much trouble from this bunch of colts, but as colts are, things are bound to happen.

And happen they did. Right in the middle of this narrow spot, one colt in the pack string blew up and started the whole mess.

The colt I was ridin' got the lead rope under his tail and was buckin' and I had no place to go. I was hangin' on just fine and lookin' for a place where I could get off 'cause it looked like the end was near. The Lord looks out for fools and children, and this must have been my day. The rope came loose and me and my pony made it through the narrows. There was just no other way we would have made it out alive. But what a mess was behind me.

Colts were hanging off the cliff. Four were dangling and four were standing on top, and my friend was wonderin' what was going to happen next.

I had made it up top and found a place to tie my pony and worked my way back down the trail to try and retrieve the rest of the colts. Meanwhile, my friend was yellin' and looking for me. He thought that I had gone over the side and was gettin' a little shook up 'cause he couldn't see through the wreck.

I soon made it back to where it all started and told him I was fine. When he saw me he started cussin' for all there was, 'cause his pony was tied to one hangin' off the cliff.

I told him to calm down, that we'd get out of this mess, that it weren't over yet. The colts seemed quieter than he did, which in this particular situation, was good.

I tied off the colts that remained on the path head and tail to some big rocks on the upper side. Then my concern went to those hangin' over the side. My next move may not have been my smartest, but I had little choice, and it was all I could think of at the time.

I made my way back to my friend so he could get off his colt. Had he not been so scared he might have been on the fight. He was still a-cussin' me, but glad to see me anyway.

We started to tie off his pony and two of the pack ponies so we could try and get the others back on top. Lucky for us, we packed a come-a-long for downed horses and it sure came in handy. (Never pack without one 'cause stuff happens. A come-a-long can haul more than a horse or a man and every now and then things just happen and it's good to have help. Hopefully for you not this bad.)

But as I was sayin', we hooked up to the horse we had tied off on top and began pullin' one colt at a time up to solid ground. It must have taken us five hours to get them all back up on the trail. But being the hands were, we got 'er done. Needless to say we had some peeled up ponies and didn't see much action from them the rest of the day.

We set up camp a good ways from the scene of the wreck. It was hard sleeping so we looked at the map to find a better way out. We sure didn't want a repeat of the day if there was a way around that place.

The next morning we found a better trail and things went pretty good. We finished our 30 days on these old colts and turned out some nice gentle ridin' horses.

My friend and I don't do this anymore. The round pen seems like a little safer place. I don't have the heart or the body anymore like I did back in those days, and now the flat land looks really good to me. But you know, miles are what make good horses and I do miss puttin' them on like I used to.

THE JACKASS, SAM, AND ME

Back when I was a boy, we lived in the hills of Oklahoma. (Yes, I said *hills* of Oklahoma.) We have some of the prettiest mountains and hills here. Most people think Oklahoma is prairie and flat, but if you look to the southeast, you will find many a mountain and hill.

My family was raised on a little farm that sat along a creek. We always had some old horses around. As kids we rode a lot and our dad taught us to break colts—he was good at that sort of thing. Dad had broken horses and mules for more than 40 years before I came along. He was a damn good hand. This how we learned to ride: He would throw us up on anything that came along, and we had to learn.

As kids we watched as he broke mules to work and horses to ride. We also saw him have many a wreck with teams, but it seemed like every time, he knew how to come out on top. Dad and Granddad raised mules to sell to the army and farmers all over the county. You could say dad had been around a might.

Dad worked away from home while my older brothers farmed with teams. They were laying corn by over in the field four or five miles from our house. My brother Sam and I were up to nothing when Momma told us to catch the jackass and take our brothers dinner.

My Dad had bought this jackass for me to learn to ride on—and learn I did. This donkey could buck, and buck he did—more times than I could shake a stick at. (Well, maybe he didn't buck; he just dropped his head and I would fall off. That's what my brothers would tell you. I said the donkey could buck.)

On this particular day, Sam and I were going to ride him to take dinner to our brothers. Sam and I thought we were real cowboys this day and doing our part to help out. The dinner Momma fixed was packed in an old lard bucket; you remember, the ones with the wire bail in it.

Getting on that donkey was not the hard part; it was after getting on that the fun began.

We had tied the lard bucket to the donkey's flank, and when he started down the road that old bucket started slapping him in the side.

I was sitting behind Sam, but in short order I found myself in front of him after the first three licks. The wreck had begun.

As the donkey bucked the bucket got louder, the bucking got harder, and soon I was behind Sam again. Next thing I knew I was eating gravel off the old dirt road. As I was bawlin' and squallin', I looked up to see Sam still a-ridin'. That bucket was still a-slapping the donkey on the flank, and soon Sam joined me on the ground a little further up the road. Seemed the only thing able to stay on that old donkey was the dinner bucket and they both disappeared over the hill.

Now Momma, hearing all the ruckus, came to investigate. She found me and Sam on the road, the donkey and dinner gone. She was none too happy with her little cowboys. Heck, she grabbed a switch on the way and used it on me for good measure.

Momma stood in the road and made us catch that old jackass. By the time we got him, the boys' dinner was pretty much gone. She was not happy with her cowboys.

She got the bucket and repacked the boys' dinner and told Sam to walk it out to the boys. I was still out of commission from being bucked off and could barely walk, let alone ride that jackass.

Sam finally talked Momma into letting him ride the jackass by himself and set the bucket in front of him. She said OK, but if it happened again she was going to switch him good and he'd still have to take the boys dinner. Sam made it after all this and dinner became supper for the boys. You might say it was late.

Probably the good Lord was looking out for our brothers. Had it not been for the buckin' and the switchin', Sam and I had planned to enjoy their dinner ourselves.

I'm glad Momma never knew that. She would have switched us for just thinkin' such a thing.

GATHERING CATTLE FOR THE BANK

One time I was gathering cattle for the bank with my nephew. These old cattle were on a place down in the mountains from where we lived. We pulled up and the old boy who owned the cattle was standing at the gate with a shotgun. I told C.P. that's what we called my nephew—we wouldn't be gathering any old cows today, at least not until the law got here.

So we stopped and parked a ways down the road, about a quarter of a mile from the gate, and here comes the old fart who owned the cattle. I tell C.P., "Hand me my gun, I'm not getting shot over the bank's cows!"

We loaded our guns and were ready for bear. That old man coming was either brave or nuts to walk up on us. We had no idea what was on his mind, and he had no way of telling what we was thinkin'. We all were in a bit of a spot.

I told C.P., "I'm going to get out and meet this man. You hold the gun on him, and if he starts shooting, let him have it." I don't know if he would have been able to let him have it—the way he was shaking, he was going to need a lot of shells; I don't think he could have hit the broad side of a barn.

I got out of the truck and walked back to talk to this old man, and he was shaking as much as C.P. I surely didn't need to get this old man excited. Either he or CP was going to shoot me, and I really didn't want to get shot.

I started talking to the old man, and before he got up to me he seemed to calm down a bit. He seemed to understand that I was on his side and didn't want to take his cows. I just worked for the bank.

The old boy said he didn't owe all that much on the cows but the bank wanted to take them all. I said, "Tell you what I'll do for you. If you will put that damn gun down, I'll call and see how much is owed and if it's like you say, we will take just enough to clear your note and leave you the rest. I won't tell if you won't. The bank don't need all your cows. They just want the money. We will give them what you owe and everyone will be happy." The old boy was happy with that.

I asked him where the cattle were and he said pointed somewhere off into the distance. Didn't leave me much to work with. I asked if he had a horse.

"A damn fine one," he spat back.

I told him to get saddled up and I would call the bank and find out how much it was going to take to get us out of there. I called and they told the tale and I explained that there was a bit of a problem. "Most of the cows," I said, "had died and we may not find the rest. But I think we can get enough to clear his note." They said OK. The old boy was satisfied and so was I.

I told him to get his horse and we unloaded ours. He had some good-looking dogs that looked like they could eat a cow up, and we took them along. I got up on my horse and met him at the gate.

"We need 15 head of good yearlings to pay you off down at the bank."

He said, "I got that and few more. So it shouldn't be that hard to fill the bill." I was thankful.

We got C.P. and headed up the trail. It was a beautiful place he had up there. We finally topped out, and as soon as we came out into the open, we could see cows everywhere. I had never seen so many damn longhorn cows. These cows had to be as old as their owner.

"As poor as these cows are we may need 20 head to fill the bill," I said. He agreed.

We started penning these crazy things, and they started running. The old boy put his dogs on them and they didn't get far. Before long we had cows, mad cows with horns, big horns—you know, the kind that you see on the hood of a Cadillac. We rode in to get around them and started pushing them to the lot. His dogs were good, but they sure did irritate them old cows. By the time we got them to the lot they were on the fight.

I told C.P., "We may have to rope about 20 head and drag them to the trailer."

While C.P. was off getting the trailer, me and the old boy lotted about 40 head. I told the old boy we would forget about the yearlings and just catch each cow and get at least 20 to 25 head and be done with it. He said that was fine with him. I told him that if there was any money left over from the sale I would see that he got it back. He was fine with this, too.

We commenced to roping whatever came by, and you ain't never seen cows fight like these did. Those horns made it a pretty sticky place to be! They would sure enough put the hook on you. My old stud was beat up and looked like he had been in fight with a bear!

As best as I can recall, we got about 23 head in all—23 head of pure hell. When we got them to the sale they ran everyone out of the ring. Mean like you have never seen. When these cows went on the fight they never came off. That was one mess I wish I had never gotten into.

Good thing cattle prices were up, otherwise the old guy would still have owed the bank. They weren't the best livestock, but they were enough to pay off his note, and he made a little bit for himself.

About three weeks later I got a thank-you note with a check inside from the old guy. He thanked me for helping him out and said anyone else would have taken all his cows. He said he liked the way we took care of him, and if he ever needed good cowboys he knew where to find them.

You know, it makes you feel good about people every now and then. Don't it?

PRAYERS

TRAVELING PRAYER

Oh, Lord,
Please look down on me,
Help me, Lord,
That I might see.

The road I travel
Seems oh so rough,
But you are with me
When the going gets tough.

Lord, let my light shine
For all the world to see,
Let them know it's you, Lord,
And not really me.

Lord, you are my Way,
My Truth and my Light,
Help me to remember this
When I lie down at night.

And forgive me, Lord,
If I may roam,
I will remember that only you
Can bring me home.

Amen

COWBOY LOOKIN' FOR A WIFE

God,

I don't come and talk too often,
But I think I need a wife.
One who will stay with me
For the rest of my life.

Lord, don't let me
Pick her this time,
'Cause I think
Your choice will do just fine.

Looking at how
I did in the past,
I found me a woman
And she just talked too fast.

Got me
To raise her kids,
And had me not knowing
That's all I did.

When the kids
Were up and gone,
Lord, she left me
All alone.

It seems I never
Put you first in my life,
I never asked for help
With this wife.

So this time around
Teach me to do right,
And send me a woman,
That I can love with all my might.

Thank you, Lord,
For giving this ol' cowboy your time,
'Cause I know you'll send me
Someone who'll do just fine.

Lord, I know you will always
Be in this heart of mine,
Always first in my life
For the rest of time.

Amen

HORSE PRAYER

Lord, let this old hoss,
Stay under me,
And keep my eyes
Where we both can see.

Let us ride 'til
Our day's work is done.
Take us home safe
From where we begun.

Lord, let me help this old hoss
When I can,
Let him know that it's my job
And I am but a hand.

Let us ride
And do our best,
Nothing more
And nothing less.

Just keep us, Lord,
Under your watchful eye,
Let us remember
All those cowboys who have died.

Safe in your hands
We all will be kept,
And we look to you
For the time we've got left.

Amen

A COWBOY WHO FINDS HIS LOVE

Lord,

I am only a cowboy
Who's found a lady of class,
I don't know what to say to her
Except she fills my glass.

Some tell me to
Take my time,
But, Lord, it's like ropin' a colt—
You can just get left behind.

I am used
To moving fast,
If you wait too long
The moment will pass.

So, Lord, help me with this lady
I think so much of,
Help me give her my heart
And all my love.

Show her I am just a cowboy
Who has a love so dear,
I will fill her needs
And do my best year after year.

Amen

A FARMER'S PRAYER

Lord, we thank you
For this rain,
And we're so glad to see
How nice it came.

Why, Lord, our old fields
Were sure 'nuf needin' the water,
And like every thing you do
You let it come when it ought to.

You are a kind
And merciful God,
And this time of year
We need it all—

All the rain
That we can get,
And, Lord,
You've never let us down yet.

Just wanted to say
Thanks to you,
For all that you have done
And all that you will do.

Amen

A COWBOY'S PRAYER FOR HIS WIFE

Now, Lord, I ain't been much
Of a husband through the years,
You know I've caused my wife
So many unnecessary tears.

I never knew
How much she meant to me,
Till she up and left,
And now I surely see.

So, Lord, help me to become the man
You would have me be,
And help me stand strong
Like the mighty oak tree.

Help me to ride
In faith for you,
And to my wife
A husband forever true.

Lord, may you see
A change in me each and every day,
Help her to put the past behind us
Whenever it gets in the way.

Lord, you know
I am not a smart man,
But I will change with your help
And you know I can.

Amen

TALKIN' WITH THE LORD

Dear Lord—

Forgive this old cowboy
Who is lookin' to you,
Who ain't much with words
But hope this will do.

We ain't seen much
Rain 'round here,
Just enough
To get us through the year.

Lord, the cattle
They are not the best,
But all in all
We sure have been blessed.

Let us thank you
For all you have done,
Help us remember
You and your Son.

I'll not take
Any more time,
'Cause long as I have you
I'll be just fine.

Amen

ANOTHER DAY

God, as I go through
Yet another day,
Give me what I need
To make it all the way.

Push my feet
Where you would have them trod,
Help me remember I am just a man
And you are my God.

Help your people
Across this land
To do their best
According to your plan.

To be kind to our children
And smile when we can,
And to do our best
To help our fellow man.

Amen

A COWBOY ON THE RANGE

Dear Lord, I don't come to you like I should,
But let me tell you how lonely sometimes I've stood.
Never lookin' up because of my shame,
Because I know without you, life ain't the same.

And, Lord, as I look on those long yesterdays,
At all these old cows as peacefully they graze,
I know it's only you
Who keeps the peace in them each day.

So, Lord, as a man why can't I have such peace of mind?
And at that moment I felt it, a peace of some kind,
God brushed his hand across my face.
God is right here with me, in this place.

I feel good inside because the rest of my life
With God I can ride.
I know God is up there in His place,
And some day I can look Him in the face.

MERCY

Dear Lord,

Have mercy on me,
For I am only a cowboy you see,
Whose life has been all uphill,
And me never doin' your will.

But, Lord, I'm here asking you now
To help me somehow.
For what I say and what I do
Got me a heap of trouble, too.

And now that I am here with you,
Help me, Lord, to change and be true.
'Cause who am I to say
How long I am here to stay?

You never ask a thing from me
Except to serve you and let it be.
'Cause mercy is where it's at,
And who am I to question that?

ABOUT THE AUTHOR

Roy Hall was born a few years back in the Oklahoma Hills he now calls home. He has two children and seven grandchildren who are the apples of his eye and whom he spoils rotten. After high school Roy went to work as a cowboy. He worked all around the country and never stayed in one place too long. He's also ridden bulls, rodeoed, worked construction, and driven trucks. He's been an underwater welder, a Voc-Tech teacher; he's worked the oilfields, he's been a mechanic, he's operated heavy equipment—and is still willing to try anything once. His first loves are still cowboying, horses, and (of course) women.

This book was written while Roy worked on ranches across this great land and is based on his own experiences from that life.

Roy has met many folks from all walks of life. He wants to put a smile on your face or a tear in your eye. His stories let us see a little of life through the eyes of this cowboy. His prayers are from the heart. Some people say horses and women are his only downfall, but he doesn't think so; he really loves them all.